GO
WITH
THE
POEM

GO WITH THE POEM

A New Collection chosen by

LILIAN MOORE

McGRAW-HILL BOOK COMPANY
New York   St. Louis   San Francisco
Montreal   Toronto

I want especially to thank
the librarians in the Public Library
of Ellenville, New York, for the
efficiency and unfailing good cheer
with which they helped me in poem
hunting for this collection.

811.5
Moo

5 8 81   10/80   7.95   B/)

Library of Congress Cataloging in Publication Data
Main entry under title:
Go with the poem
Bibliography: p.
Includes index.
Summary: A collection of some 90 poems written by
such outstanding 20th-century poets as William Carlos
Williams, Robert Frost, and Lillian Morrison.
1. Children's poetry. [1. Poetry—Collections]
I. Moore, Lilian.
PN6110.C4G659   811'.5'208   78-8393
ISBN 0-07-042880-8

Book design by Kathleen Westray

2 3 4 5 6 7 8 9 BPBP   8 3 2 1 0

ACKNOWLEDGMENTS

We gratefully acknowledge the following permissions:

A. R. Ammons. "Poem," from DIVERSIFICATIONS, Poems. Copyright © 1975 by A. R. Ammons. Reprinted by permission of W. W. Norton & Company, Inc.

Byrd Baylor. "Children of the Desert," excerpted from THE DESERT IS THEIRS. Copyright © 1975 by Byrd Baylor. Reprinted by permission of Charles Scribner's Sons and Toni Strassman, Agent.

Paul Blackburn. "The Yawn." Copyright © 1968 by Paul Blackburn. Reprinted by permission of Mrs. Joan Blackburn.

Richard Brautigan. "The Chinese Checker Players," excerpted from THE PILL VERSUS THE SPRINGHILL MINE DISASTER. Copyright © 1968 by Richard Brautigan. Reprinted by permission of Delacorte Press/Seymour Lawrence and The Brann-Hartnett Agency, Inc.

Joseph Bruchac. "Birdfoot's Grampa," from ENTERING ONONDAGA, Cold Mountain Press, Austin, Texas. Copyright © 1975 by Joseph Bruchac. Reprinted by permission of the Author.

David Budbill. "New York in the Spring," from CITY IN ALL DIRECTIONS, edited by Arnold Adoff. Reprinted by permission of the Author.

Lucille Clifton. "Eviction" (originally titled "the 1st"), and "in the inner city," from GOOD TIMES. Copyright © 1969 by Lucille Clifton. Reprinted by permission of Random House, Inc.

Theodore Clymer. "Growing Songs" (originally titled "My Great Corn Plants," Navajo Indian; "Nicely, Nicely, Nicely" and "Nicely while it is raining," Acoma Indian), from FOUR CORNERS OF THE SKY, edited by Theodore Clymer. Copyright © 1975 by Theodore Clymer. Reprinted by permission of Little, Brown and Co. in association with The Atlantic Monthly Press.

Donald Finkel. "A Cellar and an Attic" is taken from the poem "Nothing at All," from A MOTE IN HEAVEN'S EYE. Copyright © 1975 by Donald Finkel. Reprinted by permission of Atheneum Publishers.

Robert Francis. "Deep Sea Diver" (originally titled "Diver"), from COME OUT INTO THE SUN. Copyright © 1936, 1964 by Robert Francis. Reprinted by permission of The University of Massachusetts Press.

Robert Froman. "Undefeated," and "Puzzle," from STREET POEMS. Copyright © 1971 by Robert Froman. Reprinted by permission of the publishers, E. P. Dutton, and by permission of Curtis Brown, Ltd.

Robert Frost. "A Time to Talk," and "The Secret Sits," from THE POETRY OF ROBERT FROST, edited by Edward Connery Latham. Copyright © 1916, 1969 by Holt, Rinehart and Winston. Copyright © 1942, 1944 by Robert Frost. Copyright © 1970 by Lesley Frost Ballantine. Reprinted by permission of Holt, Rinehart and Winston, Publishers and Jonathan Cape Ltd., London.

Emilie Glen. "Apple Scoop." Reprinted by permission of the Author.

CONTENTS

FOR JON AND SAM

Go with the poem.
Hang glide
above new landscape
into other weather.

Sail the poem.
Lift.
Drift over treetops
and towers.

Loop with the poem.
Swoop, dip.
Land.
Where?
Trust the poem.

LILIAN MOORE

1

"I'M THE DRIVER AND THE WHEEL"

ON THE SKATEBOARD

Skimming
an asphalt sea
I swerve, I curve, I
sway; I speed to whirring
sound an inch above the
ground; I'm the sailor
and the sail, I'm the
driver and the wheel
I'm the one and only
single engine
human auto
mobile.

LILLIAN MORRISON

ON OUR BIKES

The roads to the beach
              are winding
    we glide down
              breeze-whipped
curving
          past hills of sand
    pedal and coast
                through wide smell of the sea
                old familiar sunfeel
        windwallop.

Race you to the water's edge!

LILLIAN MORRISON

RIDING LESSON

I learned two things
from an early riding teacher.
He held a nervous filly
in one hand and gestured
with the other, saying, "Listen.
Keep one leg on one side,
the other leg on the other side,
and your mind in the middle."

He turned and mounted.
She took two steps, then left
the ground, I thought for good.
But she came down hard, humped
her back, swallowed her neck,
and threw her rider as you'd
throw a rock. He rose, brushed
his pants and caught his breath,
and said, "See, that's the way
to do it. When you see
they're gonna throw you, get off."

HENRY TAYLOR

FOUL SHOT

With two 60's stuck on the scoreboard
And two seconds hanging on the clock,
The solemn boy in the center of eyes,
Squeezed by silence,
Seeks out the line with his feet,
Soothes his hands along his uniform,
Gently drums the ball against the floor
Then measures the waiting net,
Raises the ball on his right hand,
Balances it with his left,
Calms it with fingertips,
Breathes,
Crouches,
Waits,
And then through a stretching of stillness,
Nudges it upward.

The ball
Slides up and out,
Lands,
Leans,
Wobbles,
Wavers,
Hesitates,
Exasperates,
Plays it coy
Until every face begs with unsounding screams—

And then,

And then

And then,

Right before ROAR-UP,
Dives down and through.

EDWIN A. HOEY

THE NEW KID

Our baseball team never did very much,
we had me and PeeWee and Earl and Dutch.
And the Oak Street Tigers always got beat
until the new kid moved in on our street.

The kid moved in with a mitt and a bat
and an official New York Yankee hat.
The new kid plays shortstop or second base
and can outrun us all in any place.

The kid never muffs a grounder or fly
no matter how hard it's hit or how high.
And the new kid always acts quite polite,
never yelling or spitting or starting a fight.

We were playing the league champs just last week;
they were trying to break our winning streak.
In the last inning the score was one—one,
when the new kid swung and hit a home run.

A few of the kids and their parents say
they don't believe that the new kid should play.
But she's good as me, Dutch, PeeWee, or Earl,
so we don't care that the new kid's a girl.

MIKE MAKLEY

DEEP SEA DIVER

Diver go down
Down through the green
Inverted dawn
To the dark unseen
To the never day
The under night
Starless and steep
Deep beneath deep
Diver fall
And falling fight
Your weed-dense way
Until you crawl
Until you touch
Weird water land
And stand.

Diver come up
Up through the green
Into the light
The sun   the seen
But in the clutch
Of your dripping hand
Diver bring
Some uncouth thing
That we could swear
And would have sworn
Was never born
Or could ever be
Anywhere
Blaze on our sight
Make us see.

ROBERT FRANCIS

SUDDENLY

All over the fields there was ice today,
and everybody was out on skates.
It had rained through Christmas, raining away
on the snow, but then in the night the fates,
or whatever it is that decides to freeze,
had dropped the temperature twenty degrees,
and here were the fields like dinner plates
in the shine and flash of the morning sun;
and never, I think, had the kids such fun
as they had on a Christmas day plus one!

Wide fields, big fields, with not any trees:
Skate where you would, and do as you please.
It wasn't just hockey and blow your nose
and lose your mittens and freeze your toes.
It was out and beyond and away on the crust
that was ice you could bend over land you could
    trust.
It was something so wonderful, barely begun,
yet on into moonlight, to over-and-done;
it was skating where no one had skated before,
through field after field till there weren't any more.

It was something just given you—yours by right;
though perhaps you didn't deserve it, quite.

DAVID McCORD

2

"THE
TIGER
HAS
SWALLOWED
A
BLACK
SUN"

THE TIGER

The tiger
Has swallowed
A black sun,

In his cold
Cage he
Carries it still:

Black flames
Flicker through
His fur,

Black rays roar
From the centers
Of his eyes.

VALERIE WORTH

SONG OF THE DEER HUNTER

Over there, far off, he runs
With his white forefeet
Through the brush.

Over there, nearby, he runs,
With his nostrils open,
Over the bare ground.

The white tail, climbing,
Seems like a streak on the rocks.
The black tail, striding,
Seems like a crack in the rocks.

PAPAGO INDIAN

SMALL, SMALLER

I thought that I knew all there was to know
Of being small, until I saw once, black against the snow,
A shrew, trapped in my footprint, jump and fall
And jump again and fall, the hole too deep, the walls
  too tall.

RUSSELL HOBAN

MOSQUITO

Onto a boy's arm came a mosquito.
"Don't hit! Don't hit!" it hummed.
"Grandchildren have I to sing to."
"Imagine," the boy said.
"So small and yet a grandfather."

EASTERN ESKIMO

LOVE SONG FOR A JELLYFISH

How amazed I was, when I was a child,
To see your life on the sand.
To see you living in your jelly shape,
Round and slippery and dangerous.
You seemed to have fallen
Not from the rim of the sea,
But from the galaxies.
Stranger, you delighted me. Weird object of
The stinging world.

SANDRA HOCHMAN

CATS SLEEP FAT

Cats sleep fat and walk thin.
Cats, when they sleep, slump;
When they wake, stretch and begin
Over, pulling their ribs in.
Cats walk thin.

Cats wait in a lump,
Jump in a streak.
Cats, when they jump, are sleek
As a grape slipping its skin—
They have technique.
Oh, cats don't creak.
They sneak.

Cats sleep fat.
They spread out comfort underneath them
Like a good mat,
As if they picked the place
And then sat;
You walk around one
As if he were the City Hall
After that.

ROSALIE MOORE
from CATALOGUE

18

BOXER PUP

On a strong
rope,
aggressive,

restrained, you
tug
at your corner,

eager
for the bell, and
to be in,

dancing
round the ring,
belligerent in

your
gloved skin,
muscled

as if to
let fists
emerge, clenched.

GEORGE MACBETH

PETE THE PUP AT THE SEASHORE

i ran along the yellow sand
and made the sea gulls fly
i chased them down the waters edge
i chased them up the sky

i ran so hard i ran so fast
i left the spray behind
i chased the flying flecks of foam
and i outran the wind

an airplane sailing overhead
climbed when it heard me bark
i yelped and leapt right at the sun
until the sky grew dark

some little children on the beach
threw sticks and ran with me
o master let us go again
and play beside the sea

DON MARQUIS

SALAMANDER

A red salamander
so cold and so
easy to catch, dreamily

moves his delicate feet
and long tail. I hold
my hand open for him to go.

DENISE LEVERTOV
from LIVING

SEA LIONS

The satin sea lions
Nudge each other
Toward the edge
Of the pool until
They fall like
Soft boulders
Into the water,
Sink down, slide
In swift circles,
Twist together
And apart, rise again
Snorting, climb
Up slapping
Their flippers on
The wet cement:
Someone said
That in all the zoo
Only the sea lions
Seem happy.

VALERIE WORTH

3

"WHAT
SHALL
I
DO
WITH
THE
SEED?"

GROWING SONGS

My great corn plants,
Among them I walk.
I speak to them;
They hold out their hands to me.

My great squash vines,
Among them I walk.
I speak to them;
They hold out their hands to me.

NAVAJO INDIAN

Nicely, nicely, nicely, nicely there away in the east,
The rain clouds are caring for the little corn plants
As a mother takes care of her baby.

ACOMA INDIAN

Nicely while it is raining,
Corn plant, I am singing for you.
Nicely while the water is streaming
Vine plant, I am singing for you.

ACOMA INDIAN

SUMMER GRASS

Summer grass aches and whispers.

It wants something;
it calls out and sings;
it pours out wishes to the overhead stars.

The rain hears;
the rain answers;
the rain is slow coming;
the rain wets the face of the grass.

CARL SANDBURG

THE SUMMER NIGHT

The summer night
is a dark blue hammock
slung between the white pillars of day.

I lie there
cooling myself
with the straw-colored
flat round fan
of the full moon.

EVE MERRIAM

TORNADO SEASON

Wind went by with people falling out of it,
and hairpins,
and a barn door swinging without its hinges.
Grass rose in swarms along with nails.
A crow flew upsidedown,
his legs reaching skyward,
and growing longer.

ADRIEN STOUTENBERG

POEM

In a high wind the
leaves don't
fall but fly
straight out of the
tree like birds

A. R. AMMONS

THEME IN YELLOW

I spot the hills
With yellow balls in autumn.
I light the prairie cornfields
Orange and tawny gold clusters
And I am called pumpkins.
On the last of October
When dusk is fallen
Children join hands
And circle round me
Singing ghost songs
And love to the harvest moon;
I am a jack-o'-lantern
With terrible teeth
And the children know
I am fooling.

CARL SANDBURG

COLD

Cold, a character I used to know
in Wyoming, raps every night
at doors of lonely farms, moans
all night around the barn, and cracks
his knuckles late, late
at the bedroom window.

WILLIAM STAFFORD
from SOME AUTUMN CHARACTERS

THERE CAME A DAY

There came a day that caught the summer
Wrung its neck
Plucked it
And ate it.

Now what shall I do with the trees?
The day said, the day said.
Strip them bare, strip them bare.
Let's see what is really there.

And what shall I do with the sun?
The day said, the day said.
Roll him away till he's cold and small.
He'll come back rested if he comes back at all.

And what shall I do with the birds?
The day said, the day said.
The birds I've frightened, let them flit,
I'll hang out the pork for the brave tomtit.

And what shall I do with the seed?
The day said, the day said.
Bury it deep, see what it's worth.
See if it can stand the earth.

What shall I do with the people?
The day said, the day said.
Stuff them with apple and blackberry pie—
They'll love me then till the day they die.

There came this day and he was autumn.
His mouth was wide
And red as a sunset.
His tail was an icicle.

TED HUGHES

JANUARY

The days are short,
    The sun a spark
Hung thin between
    The dark and dark.

Fat snowy footsteps
    Track the floor.
Milk bottles burst
    Outside the door.

The river is
    A frozen place
Held still beneath
    The trees of lace.

The sky is low.
    The wind is gray.
The radiator
    Purrs all day.

                                        JOHN UPDIKE

THE SNOW FALL

Quietness clings to the air.
Quietness gathers the bell
To a great distance.
Listen!
This is the snow.
This is the slow
Chime
The snow
Makes.
It encloses us.
Time in the snow is alone:
Time in the snow is at last,
Is past.

ARCHIBALD MACLEISH

SPRING IS

Spring is when
    the morning sputters like
bacon
      and
        your
          sneakers
        run
         down
           the
             stairs
so fast you can hardly keep up with them,
and
spring is when
    your scrambled eggs
        jump
         off
           the
             plate
and turn into a million daffodils
trembling in the sunshine.

BOBBI KATZ

SPRING THUNDER

Listen. The wind is still,
And far away in the night—
See! The uplands fill
With a running light.

Open the doors. It is warm;
And where the sky was clear—
Look! The head of a storm
That marches here!

Come under the trembling hedge—
Fast, although you fumble.
There! Did you hear the edge
Of winter crumble?

MARK VAN DOREN

4

"WHEN
A
FRIEND
CALLS
TO
ME"

A TIME TO TALK

When a friend calls to me from the road
And slows his horse to a meaning walk,
I don't stand still and look around
On all the hills I haven't hoed,
And shout from where I am, "What is it?"
No, not as there is a time to talk.
I thrust my hoe in the mellow ground,
Blade-end up and five feet tall,
And plod: I go up to the stone wall
For a friendly visit.

ROBERT FROST

THE RAIN REMINDS ME

the rain reminds me of my father
falling asleep in the middle of a story
the warm stubble on his cheek
sleep seeping up through the cracks
in his voice; we were sleeping like
crabs in the armchair, silent in a
viking sea, and I dreamed about
eating popcorn at the animal fair.

JONATHAN MOORE

APPLE SCOOP

My Grandmother at her farm table
Would scrape an apple with a pen-knife,
Paring the skin in red curls
    Round and round,
Before scooping up the juice meat,
I never could get the art of it
But far from the orchards
    Above Lake Erie,
From her farm kitchen
    With its bowl of apples,
I try for the red curls

EMILIE GLEN

PORTRAIT

A big young bareheaded woman
in an apron

Her hair slicked back standing
on the street

One stockinged foot toeing
the sidewalk

Her shoe in her hand. Looking
intently into it

She pulls out the paper insole
to find the nail

That has been hurting her

WILLIAM CARLOS WILLIAMS

BIRDFOOT'S GRAMPA

The Old Man
must have stopped our car
two dozen times to climb out
and gather into his hands
the small toads blinded
by our lights and leaping
like live drops of rain.

The rain was falling,
a mist around his white hair,
and I kept saying,
"You can't save them all,
accept it, get in,
we've got places to go."

But, leathery hands full
of wet brown life,
knee deep in the summer
roadside grass,
he just smiled and said,
"They have places to go, too."

JOSEPH BRUCHAC

IT HAPPENED IN MONTGOMERY

One day in 1955 in Montgomery, Alabama, a black seamstress, Mrs. Rosa Parks, was ordered by a bus driver to give up her seat to a white man and move to the back of the bus. She refused and was arrested. This act inspired the Reverend Martin Luther King, Jr., to organize a massive bus boycott which was the beginning of the great Civil Rights Movement.

for Rosa Parks

Then he slammed on the brakes—
Turned around and grumbled.

But she was tired that day.
Weariness was in her bones.
And so the thing she's done yesterday,
And yesteryear,
On her workdays,
Churchdays,
Nothing-to-do-guess-I'll-go-and-visit Sister Annie
Days—

She felt she'd never do again.

And he growled once more.

So she said:
No sir . . . I'm stayin' right here.

And he gruffly grabbed her,
Pulled and pushed her—
Then sharply shoved her through the doors.

The news slushed through the littered streets
Slipped into the crowded churches,
Slimmered onto the unmagnolied side of town
While the men talked and talked and talked.

She—
Who was tired that day,
Cried and sobbed that she was glad she'd done it.
That her soul was satisfied.

That Lord knows,
A little walkin' never hurt anybody;

That in one of those unplanned, unexpected
Unadorned moments—
A weary woman turned the page of History.

PHIL W. PETRIE

FERNANDO

Fernando has a basketball.
He tap, tap, taps it down the hall,
then leaps up high and shoots with care.
The fact a basket isn't there,
he totally dismisses.
He says he never misses.
My crazy friend Fernando.

MARCI RIDLON

THE CHINESE CHECKER PLAYERS

When I was six years old
I played Chinese checkers
    with a woman
who was ninety-three years old.
She lived by herself
in an apartment down the hall
    from ours.
We played Chinese checkers
every Monday and Thursday nights.
While we played she usually talked
about her husband
who had been dead for seventy years,
and we drank tea and ate cookies
    and cheated.

RICHARD BRAUTIGAN

5

"THE
SECRET
KNOWS"

THE SHIP MOVES

The ship moves
but its smoke
moves with the wind
faster than the ship

—thick coils of it
through leafy trees
pressing
upon the river

WILLIAM CARLOS WILLIAMS

OPPOSITES

The opposite of a *cloud* could be
A white reflection in the sea,

Or a huge blueness in the air,
Caused by a cloud's not being there.

RICHARD WILBUR

NO ONE WOULD BELIEVE

No one would believe
unless they saw too
as the train passed him
           (but it's true)
facing the river
alone in the wind
an old old man
playing violin.

          CHARLOTTE ZOLOTOW

from WATER PICTURE

In the pond in the park
all things are doubled:
Long buildings hang and
wriggle gently. Chimneys
are bent legs bouncing
on clouds below. A flag
wags like a fishhook
down there in the sky.

MAY SWENSON

WHICH

Which of the horses
we passed yesterday whinnied
all night in my dreams?
I want that one.

WILLIAM STAFFORD

WHAT ARE YOU DOING?

What are you doing in our street among the automobiles,
horse?
How are your cousins, the centaur and the unicorn?

CHARLES REZNIKOFF

DINOSAURS

Their feet, planted into tar,
drew them down,
back to the core of birth,
and all they are
is found in earth,
recovered, bone by bone,
rising again, like stone
skeletons, naked, white,
to live again, staring,
head holes glaring,
towering, proud, tall,
in some museum hall.

MYRA COHN LIVINGSTON

THE SECRET SITS

We dance round in a ring and suppose
But the Secret sits in the middle and knows.

ROBERT FROST

A CELLAR AND AN ATTIC

A cellar and an attic are friends
the cellar works hard for his keep
and has for his pains a furnace in his throat
and a bellyful of boiling water
the attic sits in the clouds from morning to night
with nothing at all in his head
but a rocking horse and a broken chair

DONALD FINKEL
from *NOTHING AT ALL*

from MUSHROOMS

So many of us!
So many of us!

We are shelves, we are
Tables, we are meek,
We are edible.

Nudgers and shovers
In spite of ourselves
Our kind multiplies.

We shall by morning
Inherit the earth.
Our foot's in the door.

SYLVIA PLATH

6

THE CITY: "WE CALL IT HOME"

OIL SLICK

There, by the curb,
a leaky truck
has drooled
a grease-pool,

a black, pearly
slick
which rainbows
when the sun
strikes it.

I could spend
all day
marbling
its flashy colors
with a stick.

JUDITH THURMAN

UNDEFEATED

little   square   of   earth

sidewalk   forgot   to   cover.

Lost.

Alone.

weeds start coming up.

ROBERT FROMAN

RAIN

Rain hits over and over
on hot tin,
on trucks,
on wires and roses.
Rain hits apples, birds, people,
coming in strokes of white,
gray, sometimes purple.
Rain cracks against my eyelids,
runs blue on my fingers,
and my shadow floats on the sidewalk
through trees and houses.

ADRIEN STOUTENBERG

THE YAWN

The black-haired girl
With the big
                brown

                        eyes
on the Queens train coming
                in to work, so
opens her mouth so beautifully
                wide
                        in a ya-aawn, that
two stops after she has left the train
I have only to think of her and i

                                o-oh-aaaww-hm
                                wow !

                                PAUL BLACKBURN

ZEBRA

white sun
black
fire escape,

morning
grazing like a zebra
outside my window.

JUDITH THURMAN

NEW YORK IN THE SPRING

Sometimes when I
am walking down the street
early in May
late in the afternoon
after it's rained
on the first hot day
of the hot summer
when the sidewalk
is still wet
and the grass smells new
the way it won't soon

When the dust is mud
and the sidewalk darkens
from the water
and the sun's not out yet
and it's cool and good
to be walking outside
after the rain

Before the dust flies in my face
and the sidewalk turns
white again
and so hot
it hurts my feet
right through my shoes
and reminds me about
the hot summer
and the sweat
and no cool air to breathe
and nowhere to go
away from the heat.

Before that

Before I take
another step
into the sun

For a moment
for a second

When the city smells cool

I forget about the space
between my teeth and I
laugh with my mouth open.

DAVID BUDBILL

THE HOUSE-WRECKERS

The house-wreckers have left the door and a staircase,
now leading to the empty room of night.

CHARLES REZNIKOFF

EVICTION

What I remember about that day
is boxes stacked across the walk
and couch springs curling through the air
and drawers and tables balanced on the curb
and us, hollering,
leaping up and around
happy to have a playground;

nothing about the empty rooms
nothing about the emptied family

LUCILLE CLIFTON

SHOESHINE MEN

who knows
if the old men
who shine shoes on the Staten Island Ferry
carry their world
in a box slung across their shoulders
if they share their lunch
with birds
flying back and forth
upon an endless journey
if they ever find their way
back home.

AUDRE LORDE
from *A TRIP ON THE STATEN ISLAND FERRY*

PUZZLE

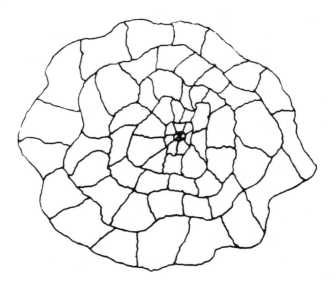

Map of a city with streets meeting at center?

Net to catch people jumping from a burning building?

Spider's web?

Burner on an electric stove?

Fingerprint?

No.

Frozen puddle after a hit by a rock.

ROBERT FROMAN

IN THE INNER CITY

in the inner city
or
like we call it
home
we think a lot about uptown
and the silent nights
and the houses straight as
dead men
and the pastel lights
and we hang on to our no place
happy to be alive
and in the inner city
or
like we call it
home

LUCILLE CLIFTON

7

"PUT
IT
TOGETHER;
THE
WORLD'S
LIKE
THAT
TOO"

JIGSAW PUZZLE

My beautiful picture of pirates and treasure
Is spoiled, and almost I don't want to start
To put it together; I've lost all the pleasure
I used to find in it: there's one missing part.

I know there's one missing—they lost it, the others,
The last time they played with my puzzle—and maybe
There's more than one missing: along with the brothers
And sisters who borrow my toys there's the baby.

There's a hole in the ship or the sea that it sails on,
And I said to my father, "Well, what shall I do?
It isn't the same now that some of it's gone."
He said, "Put it together; the world's like that too."

RUSSELL HOBAN

BEE

A bee thumps against the dusty window,
falls to the sill,
climbs back up, buzzing;
falls again;
and does this over and over.
If only he would climb higher!
The top half of the window is
open.

ROBERT SUND

BEWARE OF ME!

i stand on the rock
ho, bear!
beware of me!

i stand on the tree
ho, eagle!
beware of me!

i stand on the mountain
ho, enemy!
beware of me!

i stand in the camp
ho, chiefs!
beware of me!

here comes a bee!
i run and hide!
he would sting me!

CHEROKEE INDIAN

SAMUEL

I found this salamander
Near the pond in the wood.
Samuel, I called him—
Samuel, Samuel.
Right away I loved him.
He loved me too, I think.
Samuel, I called him—
Samuel, Samuel.

I took him home in a coffee can,
And at night
He slept in my bed.
In the morning
I took him to school.

He died very quietly during spelling.

Sometimes I think
I should have left him
Near the pond in the woods.
Samuel, I called him—
Samuel, Samuel.

BOBBI KATZ

EIGHTEEN FLAVORS

Eighteen luscious, scrumptious flavors—
Chocolate, lime and cherry,
Coffee, pumpkin, fudge-banana,
Caramel cream and boysenberry.
Rocky road and toasted almond,
Butterscotch, vanilla dip,
Butter-brickle, apple ripple,
Coconut and mocha chip,
Brandy peach and lemon custard,
Each scoop lovely, smooth, and round,
Tallest ice-cream cone in town,
Lying there (sniff) on the ground.

SHEL SILVERSTEIN

ACCIDENTALLY

Once—I didn't mean to,
but that
was that—
I yawned in the sunshine
and swallowed a gnat.

I'd rather eat mushrooms
and bullfrogs' legs,
I'd rather have pepper
all over my eggs

than open my mouth
on a sleepy day
and close on a gnat
going down that way.

It tasted sort of salty.
It didn't hurt a bit.
I accidentally ate a gnat
and that
was
it!

MAXINE W. KUMIN

HOMEWORK

Homework sits on top of Sunday, squashing Sunday flat.
Homework has the smell of Monday, homework's very fat
Heavy books and piles of paper, answers I don't know.
Sunday evening's almost finished, now I'm going to go
Do my homework in the kitchen. Maybe just a snack,
Then I'll sit right down and start as soon as I run back
For some chocolate sandwich cookies. Then I'll really do
All that homework in a minute. First I'll see what new
Show they've got on television in the living room.
Everybody's laughing there, but misery and gloom
And a full refrigerator are where I am at.
I'll just have another sandwich. Homework's very fat.

RUSSELL HOBAN

"INVISIBLE MESSAGES"

MAGNET

This small
Flat horseshoe
Is sold for
A toy: we are
Told that it
Will pick up pins
And it does, time
After time; later
It lies about,
Getting its red
Paint chipped, being
Offered pins less
Often, until at
Last we leave it
Alone: then
It leads its own
Life, trading
Secrets with
The North Pole,
Reading
Invisible messages
From the sun.

VALERIE WORTH

ALL THE SMOKE

All the smoke
Rising
From McKeesport, Pa.,
On an afternoon
In twilight,
Weighs
Two pounds, net.

ELI SIEGEL

NOTE

straw, feathers, dust—
little things

but if they all go one way,
that's the way the wind goes.

WILLIAM STAFFORD

ROCKS

Big rocks into pebbles,
pebbles into sand.
I really hold a million million rocks here in my hand.

FLORENCE PARRY HEIDE

FLASHLIGHT

My flashlight tugs me
through the dark
like a hound
with a yellow eye,

sniffs
at the edges
of steep places,

paws
at moles'
and rabbits'
holes,

points its nose
where sharp things
lie asleep—

and then it bounds
ahead of me
on home ground.

JUDITH THURMAN

ALARM CLOCK

in the deep sleep forest
there were ferns
there were feathers
there was fur
and a soft ripe peach
on a branch within my
r-r-r-r-r-r-r-r-r-r-r-r-r-r-r-r-r-r-

EVE MERRIAM

A GRANDFATHER POEM

A grandfather poem
must use words of great dignity.

It can not
contain words like:
Ubangi
rolling pin
popsicle,

but words like:
Supreme Court
graceful
wise.

WILLIAM J. HARRIS

THE MICROSCOPE

Anton Leeuwenhoek was Dutch.
He sold pincushions, cloth and such.
The waiting townsfolk fumed and fussed
As Anton's dry goods gathered dust.

He worked instead of tending store,
At grinding special lenses for
A microscope. Some of the things
He looked at were:

                mosquitoes' wings,
the hairs of sheep, the legs of lice,
the skin of people, dogs and mice;
ox eyes, spiders' spinning gear,
fishes' scales, a little smear
of his own blood,

            and best of all,
the unknown, busy, very small
bugs that swim and bump and hop
inside a simple water drop.

Impossible! Most Dutchmen said.
This Anton's crazy in the head.
We ought to ship him off to Spain.
He says he's seen a housefly's brain.
He says the water that we drink
Is full of bugs. He's mad, we think!

They called him dumkopf, which means dope.
That's how we got the microscope.

MAXINE KUMIN

96

"A
RHYME
FOR
W"

W

The King sent for his wise men all
    To find a rhyme for W;
When they had thought a good long time
But could not think of a single rhyme,
    'I'm sorry,' said he, 'to trouble you.'

JAMES REEVES

GLOWWORM

Never talk down to a glowworm—
Such as *What do you knowworm?*
How's it down belowworm?
Guess you're quite a slowworm.
No. Just say
                Helloworm!

DAVID McCORD

LUMPS

Humps are lumps
and so are mumps.

Bumps make lumps
on heads.

Mushrooms grow
in clumps of lumps—
on clumps of stumps,
in woods and dumps.

Springs spring lumps
in beds.

Mosquito bites
make itchy lumps.

Frogs on logs
make twitchy lumps.

JUDITH THURMAN

THE PANTHER

The panther is like a leopard,
Except it hasn't been peppered.
Should you behold a panther crouch,
Prepare to say Ouch.
Better yet, if called by a panther,
Don't anther.

OGDEN NASH

THE GUPPY

Whales have calves.
Cats have kittens.
Bears have cubs,
Bats have bittens,
Swans have cygnets,
Seals have puppies,
But guppies just have little guppies.

OGDEN NASH

THE TICKLE RHYME

"Who's that tickling my back?" said the wall.
    "Me," said a small
Caterpillar. "I'm learning
To crawl."

IAN SERRAILLIER

BOOKWORM

A bookworm of curious breed
Took a bite of a book out of greed
    When he found it was tasty,
    He said, "I've been hasty.
I think I shall learn how to read."

MARY ANN HOBERMAN

THE ACROBATS

I'll swing
By my ankles,
She'll cling
To your knees
As you hang
By your nose
From a high-up
Trapeze.
But just one thing, please,
As we float through the breeze—
Don't sneeze.

SHEL SILVERSTEIN

IF I HAD A BRONTOSAURUS

If I had a brontosaurus,
I would name him Horace or Morris.
But if suddenly one day he had
A lot of little brontosauri—
I would change his name
To Laurie.

SHEL SILVERSTEIN

10

"OUR
MOTHER
THE
EARTH,
OUR
FATHER
THE
SKY"

SONG OF THE SKY LOOM

Oh our Mother the Earth oh our Father the Sky
Your children are we
    with tired backs we bring you the gifts you love

So weave for us a garment of brightness

May the warp be the white light of morning
May the weft be the red light of evening
May the fringes be the falling rain
May the border be the standing rainbow

Weave for us this bright garment
that we may walk where birds sing
    where grass is green

Oh our Mother the Earth oh our Father the Sky

TEWA INDIAN,
translated by Herbert Spinden

SUN

The sun
Is a leaping fire
Too hot
To go near,

But it will still
Lie down
In warm yellow squares
On the floor

Like a flat
Quilt, where
The cat can curl
And purr.

VALERIE WORTH

MOON

The moon was but a chin of gold
    A night or two ago,
And now she turns her perfect face
    Upon the world below.

EMILY DICKINSON

STORM

In a storm,
the wind talks
with its mouth wide open.
It yells around corners
with its eyes shut.
It bumps into itself
and falls over a roof
and whispers
OH . . . Oh . . . oh . . . .

ADRIEN STOUTENBERG

NIGHT

A wolf
I considered myself
but
the owls are hooting
and
the night I fear.

OSAGE INDIAN

from CHILDREN OF THE DESERT

This is no place
for anyone
who wants
soft hills
and meadows
and everything
green
green
green . . .

This is for hawks
that like only
the loneliest canyons
and lizards
that run
in the hottest sand
and
coyotes
that choose
the rockiest trails.

It's for them.

And for
birds
that nest
in cactus
and sing out over
a thousand thorns
because
they're where
they want to be.

It's for them.

And for
hard skinny plants
that do without water
for months
at a time.

BYRD BAYLOR

LAYING THE DUST

What a sweet smell rises
      when you lay the dust—
bucket after bucket of water thrown
on the yellow grass.
            The water
flashes
each time you
make it leap—
      arching its glittering back.
The sound of
         more water
pouring into the pail
almost quenches my thirst.
Surely when flowers
grow here, they'll not
smell sweeter than this
      wet ground, suddenly black.

DENISE LEVERTOV

DAYBREAK IN ALABAMA

When I get to be a composer
I'm gonna write me some music about
Daybreak in Alabama
And I'm gonna put the purtiest songs in it
Rising out of the ground like a swamp mist
And falling out of heaven like soft dew.
I'm gonna put some tall tall trees in it
And the scent of pine needles
And the smell of red clay after rain
And long red necks
And poppy colored faces
And big brown arms
And the field daisy eyes
Of black and white black white black people
And I'm gonna put white hands
And black hands and brown and yellow hands
And red clay earth hands in it
Touching everybody with kind fingers
And touching each other natural as dew
In that dawn of music when I
Get to be a composer
And write about daybreak
In Alabama.

LANGSTON HUGHES

INDEX